writing
character

A Book of Writing Prompts

the san francisco writers' grotto
authors of *642 Things to Write About*

foreword by Constance Hale

ABRAMS NOTERIE, NEW YORK

writing character

Once, in a trattoria in Livorno, an Italian painter drew my face on a napkin. I noticed him laboring over my forehead. "Do you frown a lot?" he inquired, looking into my eyes and then pointing at the lines between my eyebrows. "Have you suffered much sadness?"

Thankfully, I've lived through no more sadness than most, but I do frown a lot—whether in impatience, frustration, or great concentration.

That moment with Aldo Matteotti taught me something about myself, but more importantly, it showed me a few things about writing.

Matteotti was forever sketching the faces he saw. Soon after this incident, in a paper store in Siena, I bought my first character journal. It would be dedicated to drawing faces (and other body parts), but in words. In the sketches that filled that book, and then in many others, I translated the painter's practice into a writer's practice. I started quietly observing the remarkable faces around me—in bars, on the bus, in the bleachers. I experimented with how to give readers a picture of a person. I searched for words to paint a precise image. And I played with metaphors, using physical details to convey psychological ones.

Most writers who consider themselves storytellers— whether they are poets, novelists, journalers, or journalists— know that characters are key to any great yarn. Spellbinding narrative almost always relies on compelling characters. For minor characters, we may have only a few words to make an impression. For major characters, the deft "character sketch" must become a deeper description that lays the groundwork for dramas to come.

Whatever the story, faces are the first portals to character.

To convey character, begin with acute observation, something we all have at our immediate disposal but rarely employ. When I say acute, I mean concentrated, focused, intent.

Stop to really look at the person you intend to describe. Think of this as "slow observation." Write down everything you notice: height, hair, shape of face, color of eyes, pallor of skin. But don't stop there. What texture is the hair? What style is the haircut? Is the person tall, six foot three, willowy, lanky, commanding, or Amazonian? What brand of shoes does he wear? What shade of blue is her hoodie? What is the sound of the person's voice?

Beware the tendency to do this too quickly and superficially. I once told an author he needed to distinguish each of the medical doctors in a book manuscript by adding quick character sketches. He tried, but the descriptions he came up with didn't make the docs stand out. They were all "tall, dark, and bearded" or "tall and bearded, with salt-and-pepper hair" or "tall, gray, and distinguished." Nice try, I told him. No cigar.

Sketches in a character journal allow you to develop the muscles you'll flex when you write a story for publication. Fans of *The New Yorker* will be familiar with the one-paragraph-long physical description that usually appears on the first or second page of the magazine's classic profiles and often focuses on the face. Here's a personal favorite, by Whitney Balliett, of jazzman Dizzy Gillespie:

> Gillespie, who is not a clotheshorse, was wearing a Sherlock Holmes hat, and houndstooth jacket, rumpled striped brown pants, a navy-blue T-shirt, and a couple of medallions suspended from a long gold neck chain. He hasn't changed much in the last ten years. He has a medium-length grayish Afro, and he looks grizzly. His huge and celebrated cheeks are broadsides in repose and spinnakers in action, and he has a scimitar smile and a thousand tiny, even teeth. He likes to smile and roll his eyes in mock surprise, but most of the time his eyes are narrowed; they take in much and send out little, and when he puts on his dark-rimmed, two-ton glasses they disappear.

Balliett's images give us a clear snapshot of the musician. Balliett starts with Gillespie's duds, focusing next on the jewelry, the cheeks, the mouth, and finally the eyes. The perfectly pitched metaphors (cheeks that are "broadsides in repose and spinnakers in action") animate the portrait. Take time to study descriptions like this to see how, exactly, the writer captures details that convey character.

Even though novelists are inventing characters, they must still give attention to detail and precise language. Louise Erdrich, in the novel *LaRose*, manages to portray several different characters by focusing, more or less, on face, height, and hair:

> The eighteen girls trying out for the team wore ponytails centered high on the back of their heads, and wide stretchy headbands of every color. Some looked Indian, some looked

maybe Indian, some looked white. Diamond grinned at Maggie. Six feet tall and in full makeup, she danced around, excited, snapping gum. Another girl's ponytail, even tightened up high, hung nearly to her waist. She was powwow royalty. Regina Sailor was her name. Snow was five feet ten and her ponytail was also long—halfway down her back. Maggie decided to grow her hair out. Diamond was powerfully muscled and the powwow princess had extremely springy crow-hop legs. Maggie decided to work out more.

Great character descriptions give us hard information ("six feet tall"; "five feet ten") as well as ideas, whether lofty ("powwow royalty") or low ("snapping gum"). Erdrich conveys character even through the names she has chosen: Diamond is flashy; Regina is queenlike. The writing is spare. Notice how the succinct last line tells us that Maggie is looking to these girls as examples of how to be. Erdrich mixes physical traits and psychological ones, looking for ways to embed the psychological in the physical.

Most of us, if we close our eyes, can conjure an image of the actor Harrison Ford. But that doesn't mean we can describe him well. To do so requires some hard looking, some deep thinking, and some careful crafting. Dave Kehr, in the *New York Times*, did all three, and he goes beyond literal description, finding metaphors:

If America had a face, it would be Harrison Ford's. It is a comfortable, creased, familiar face, a face of no particular ethnicity (Mr. Ford's father was of Irish Catholic descent, his mother Russian Jewish) and no particular region (Mr. Ford grew up in Park Ridge, Ill., a nondescript, middle-class suburb of

Chicago). It is the face of someone you know and always have known—a solid, stalwart person, someone who can be relied on to do a good job, to be a good husband, to bring up good kids. It's a face for cereal boxes and dollar bills, the face of someone you would select, as Mr. Ford was recently, to read excerpts from the Declaration of Independence during the national broadcast of Macy's Fourth of July fireworks.

But there's something else in that face—something in the eyes that's fearful and easily hurt, something in the off-angled mouth that's sardonic, even a bit cruel. The disarming, boyish smile shades into a sneer with only the tiniest twist of a facial muscle.

Kehr starts with the generic noun *face*, but he also gives us very specific ethnicity (Irish Catholic, Russian Jewish) and geography (Park Ridge, Illinois). These details come from careful reporting, but they work figuratively as well as literally: Both the ethnic mix and the Midwestern hometown say "all-American." This is the face of "a solid, stalwart person"—a good husband and a good father. Again, the writer is thinking figuratively; his nouns and adjectives spring from creativity and maybe a thesaurus. Then the concrete nouns of the physical world give way to one idea after another: We get fear, hurt, sardonicism, cruelty, and a sneer.

To enliven your writing, follow Kehr's lead and leave the world of the literal to play around in the figurative. Stop and ask yourself a few questions that will allow you to think of characters in a more metaphorical way:

If this character were a color, which color would he be?

If this character were a car, which car would she be?

What animal does this character move like, and is there a verb for that?

The journalist George Packer answers the question "What animal does this character resemble?" in an article describing characters in the US Capitol: "Observed from the press gallery, the senators in their confined space began to resemble zoo animals—[Carl] Levin a shambling brown bear, John Thune a loping gazelle, Jim Bunning a maddened grizzly." By using metaphors, Packer gives the reader a vivid image of each senator, but he conveys personality, too.

As you build a picture of someone, you want to get under his or her skin. You are interested in the mix of emotions, drives, history, and secrets that make up each of us. (I always say that a character sketch isn't done until I've sensed the paradox of the person. Everyone, after all, is a walking contradiction.)

Here's a sketch that started in my own character journal, after I encountered an ingenuous young man on a flight home to California from Hawai'i:

Met Johnny at the gate in Honolulu: twenty years old, mixed-race (black, American Indian, and some sort of white), bean-pole-like, fetching combination of wide-eyed curiosity and hard-luck stories, naive and street-smart. He was raised in Berkeley, went to Malcolm X Elementary, worked at Johnson's barbershop on Sacramento, went to Hawai'i to cut hair with his uncle, had his brand-new equipment robbed, was heading home to get his old equipment and see his three-day-old brother. He wants to go back to Honolulu, where he and his uncle cut hair "off of Likelike." I sensed something truly sweet about him, answered his funny questions about Hawaiian history ("Is it true they had warriors, but the white man had guns?"), gave him a brief history of Lili'uokalani, told him to visit 'Iolani Palace when he goes back, took a gamble and offered him a ride home. Bruce was dubious, but then was as taken in as I had been. We left Johnny at his mother's house, where a pink Karmann Ghia and a VW bus painted with flowers were standing guard. He put Bruce's number into one of his two iPhones—the work phone—and told Bruce he'd give him a haircut anytime, "cheaper than Supercuts, and better."

Immediately after I met Johnny, I wrote down snippets about him, starting with concrete details that captured character (his age, his ethnicity, his beanpole body) and quotes that captured his real voice. I settled on some plot details that suggested the contours and struggles of his life. Then I started to play with contradictions—the surprise of the pink Karmann Ghia and "something truly sweet," which came through his eagerness to see his baby brother and his offer of a haircut. Finally, in rewriting, I tried to articulate the paradox of him, his "combination of wide-eyed curiosity and hard-luck stories, naive and street-smart."

A great character sketch is an honorable act. You are trying to get to something true, even if it's not entirely polite. I once wrote this sketch of two men who called each other, somewhat facetiously, Mick—the contractor Michael John, who was Irish, and his sidekick John Michael, who was English. Clients called them Irish Mick and English Mick, or just the Micks. In other hands, they might've been described as exactly alike, with the same generic words. That would've dishonored the unique humanity of each character:

> Irish Mick is tall and reedy with skin so paper-thin you can see the blue veins on his hands. You won't see him in winter without a tight-knit wool cap; in summer, he shaves his dark hair close to the skin. He has green eyes, a fine, delicate, lady's nose, and, in the morning, the shakes. He's a type you want to take care of. Each December, he designs sets for an Irish troupe's Christmas play, performed in pubs around town.
>
> English Mick is stocky, with a pockmarked face and steel-gray hair cut spiky on top. He has three kids by two different women, one an artist in Northampton; his current girl is a Pilates instructor. He wears square-cut wire-framed glasses or tortoise-shell oval ones, and likes Emmylou Harris, gourmet food, and detective novels. ("What's this?" he said, his eye catching a copy of *Shake the Devil Off: A True Story of the Murder That Rocked New Orleans* as he walked toward my kitchen to inspect a pipe. He read it in two nights flat.) He manages to say "fuck" a lot, twisted into "fock" by his Northern English accent.
>
> Irish Mick is the loquacious one, his County Cork voice shaping vowels the way he wants them. The guy from Benin, on the second floor, is named Hugues, rhymes with "moog." Mick calls him Og, rhymes with "hog." Me, he calls "darlin'," emphasis on the "daarrrr." Steve, the neurologist on the first floor, he calls "Steve." Or "aaasshole."

A simple sketch of a face can turn into a poetic vignette, a chapter, a novel. If you tune in to a character's voice, you get more detail, and maybe even a snippet of dialogue. Putting a person in a context, or a scene, allows us to use character to get at the human condition.

And the writer himself, or herself in my case, enters into the character sketch. Dave Kehr was putting his own insights into his portrait of Harrison Ford, projecting emotional qualities onto the protean face of the actor. This is writing as an act of emotional intelligence. But the narrator can also be a character in the drama. I used the first person in sketching Johnny, partly because it allowed me to show his ingenuousness as well as his generosity. In my description of the Micks, my presence is a little more subtle, but the interaction of writer and subject can add dimension to a character portrayal.

In every character description, every word must count, and tension is valuable. Character descriptions that are expansive and compassionate are deeply satisfying. But expansive doesn't mean long. Poets reign when it comes to this ability to rely on few words to convey much.

The poet Ai Ogawa writes spare, uncompromising lines that give voice to disenfranchised characters and difficult subject matter. In "Woman to Man," she uses an image of a face illuminated by lightning to get at human contradictions both private and public:

> . . . your face, the fan, folds up,
> so I won't see how afraid
> to be with me you are.
> We don't mix, even in bed,

where we keep ending up.
There's no need to hide it:
you're snow, I'm coal,
I've got the scars to prove it.

Not all poetic portraits are so stark, but poets are proof that the more you write, the better you become at doing more with less.

The same holds true for Picasso. The young Picasso (age nine or so) started off with life drawing and detailed portraits. As he matured, he did more with less. He never stopped working to remove extraneous detail and weight from his drawings and prints. Perhaps the most famous is his *Partial Female Figure* from 1931. That one took only four lines.

That character journal I bought after meeting Aldo Matteotti in a trattoria in Italy? It's full. So are the many dozens of journals I've purchased since. They've led to articles and biographies and this essay. Consider the blank pages in this book your character journal now. Find a nearby person and start sketching.

....

CONSTANCE HALE is an American writer and critic based in San Francisco. Her work has appeared in newspapers and magazines around the country, and she has written a biography of the hula master Patrick Makuakāne. But she is best known for her books on craft: *Sin and Syntax; Vex, Hex, Smash, Smooch*; and *Wired Style*. She has taught writing and editing at Harvard and UC Berkeley.

writing character: a summary

- **Practice acute observation.** Slow down and take in all the details of your subject; experiment with writing physical descriptions that are essentially portraits drawn with words—and be extremely specific.

- **Link physical features to psychological ones.** Instead of saying "he's shy," describe how your character carries himself, his body language, and what he wears. How are your character's physical traits representative of his or her personality and state of mind?

- **Enliven your characters through metaphor.** This works two ways: (a) Use metaphor in your physical descriptions (see the Dizzy Gillespie example by Whitney Balliett). (b) Think about your character as a metaphor for a larger concept or abstract idea (revisit the Harrison Ford example by Dave Kehr).

- **Honor the complexity of your character.** Pay attention to paradox that is present in every person. Resist the temptation to weed out contradictions.

- **Think of your narrator as a character.** The voice describing the other characters in a story is rarely neutral and characterless. Think about your narrator's attitude and point of view and how it colors your character descriptions.

- **Do more with less.** Work on being as economical as possible with all the approaches above. Refine your word choice until you have your character sketched with just a few precisely selected words.

writing prompts

To get yourself going, make a list of words that describe the physical traits of one of your family members (starting with the face and working your way down). Use a thesaurus. Consult a dictionary. You can string the words together into artful sentences later.

words for _____

portrait of _____

Working with your list of words on the previous page, "draw" your family member from top to bottom. Start with the face and then move on to describe the rest of the body, including clothing, carriage, and gestures.

_____

_____

_____

_____

_____

_____

_____

_____

_____

_____

_____

_____

_____

_____

_____

_____

_____

_____

_____

_____

study a stranger

Go to a public place and observe someone for a while. This exercise works best if the person is someone who interacts with others, such as a barista, server, bus driver, or parent at the playground.

What adjectives describe this person's physical presence? (Catlike? Shrinking? Ebullient?)

_____

_____

_____

_____

What verbs describe the way this person moves? (Slinks? Lopes? Storms in?)

_____

_____

_____

_____

What verbs describe the way this person talks? (Mutters? Flirts? Condescends?)

_____

_____

_____

_____

Write a few sentences that convey the personality of your observed character, without stating things like "she is confident" or "he is jaded."

_____

_____

_____

_____

_____

_____

_____

Now flesh out your character with interior monologue; imagine what this person is thinking or feeling.

_____

_____

_____

_____

_____

_____

_____

_____

Make a list of all the words you can think of to describe hair. Think about color, texture, personality-driven characteristics (unruly, coiffed), and metaphorical ones (stringy, leonine).

brunette, bun, bouncy

_____   _____
_____   _____
_____   _____
_____   _____
_____   _____
_____   _____
_____   _____
_____   _____
_____   _____
_____   _____
_____   _____
_____   _____
_____   _____
_____   _____
_____   _____
_____   _____
_____   _____
_____   _____
_____   _____
_____   _____
_____   _____

hair, hair, everywhere

Write a scene in a barbershop or a salon, introducing a series of characters with descriptions that focus primarily on each person's hair.

cropped, tousled, tossed

How do your characters style their hair, and what does it reveal about their personalities? Consider how the clients talk about their hair or physically engage with it (touching it, tossing it). Alternatively, focus on the stylists or barbers: Can you sketch their characters based on how they handle their clients' hair?

a shift in mood

Using a few small physical actions and facial descriptions, transform a person's mood from happy to sad.

_____

_____

_____

_____

_____

_____

_____

_____

_____

_____

_____

_____

_____

_____

_____

_____

_____

_____

_____

_____

_____

Using a few small physical actions and facial descriptions, transform a person's mood from bad to good.

_____

_____

_____

_____

_____

_____

_____

_____

_____

_____

_____

_____

_____

_____

_____

_____

_____

make like a playwright

In 250 words, record all the shifts in a character's face while he's delivering a monologue.

_____

_____

_____

_____

_____

_____

_____

_____

_____

_____

_____

monologue suggestions

Having trouble coming up with a subject for your character? Try one of these:

- Explain a missed deadline.

- Justify an expensive purchase.

- Propose marriage.

- Give care instructions for a pet rattlesnake.

- Harangue a roommate for opening your mail.

- Scream about a bee.

Make a list of all the words you can think of to describe noses. Think about shape and size, the noises and movements of noses (sniffling, nostril-flaring), metaphorical descriptions (snout, beak), and expressions involving noses (turning up one's nose).

freckled, ski slope, beak

the nose knows

Create a character whose nose is either essential to his job (such as a sommelier or perfumer) or central to a task at hand (cooking or cleaning out the fridge). Write a small scene in which the nose tells us essential things about this character.

_____

_____

_____

_____

_____

_____

_____

_____

_____

_____

_____

_____

_____

_____

_____

_____

_____

_____

_____

Make a list of words that describe
your own physical traits. Be as specific
as possible, and use a thesaurus or
a visual dictionary to broaden the
vocabulary that you use for yourself.
Start with your face and then move
on to your body and gestures.

words for myself

_____   _____
_____   _____
_____   _____
_____   _____
_____   _____
_____   _____
_____   _____
_____   _____
_____   _____
_____   _____
_____   _____
_____   _____
_____   _____
_____   _____
_____   _____
_____   _____
_____   _____
_____   _____
_____   _____
_____   _____
_____   _____
_____   _____

shade it this way, then that way

Use the following prompts to practice writing about yourself from different points of view.

Describe yourself in the third person; be self-deprecating.

_____

_____

_____

_____

_____

Describe yourself in the third person; be grandiose in outlook.

_____

_____

_____

_____

_____

Describe yourself just by the way you use your hands.

_____

_____

_____

_____

_____

Describe yourself by the way you greet people.

_____

_____

_____

_____

_____

Go to the gym. Describe your physical sensations in the first few seconds of the workout.

_____

_____

_____

_____

_____

Describe yourself as the person on the next treadmill sees you.

_____

_____

_____

_____

_____

_____

portrait of authority

Choose an authority figure in your life (a boss, teacher, parent—preferably someone you can observe). What's her level of authority and how does she signal it? Write a scene demonstrating how this character wields power through speech, body language, and other physical attributes.

_____

_____

_____

_____

_____

_____

_____

_____

_____

_____

_____

_____

_____

_____

_____

_____

_____

_____

_____

_____

_____

_____

the famous face

Describe a famous person—someone you admire or feel strongly about. Avoid cliché. Go beyond literal description and use metaphor to communicate what this person signifies to you.

_____

_____

_____

_____

_____

_____

_____

_____

_____

_____

_____

_____

_____

_____

_____

_____

_____

_____

personal artifacts

Describe a roommate, coworker, or family member based
entirely on the objects arranged on his or her desk or dresser.

_____

_____

_____

_____

_____

_____

_____

_____

_____

_____

_____

_____

_____

_____

_____

_____

_____

_____

_____

_____

itemization

Find a shopping list, receipt, or credit card statement (yours or, if possible, someone else's). Write a character sketch inspired by the items on that list.

we are so complicated

Write about the positive aspects of someone you loathe.

_____

_____

_____

_____

_____

_____

_____

_____

_____

_____

_____

_____

_____

_____

_____

_____

_____

_____

_____

_____

_____

_____

_____

Write about the negative aspects of someone you love.

_____

_____

_____

_____

_____

_____

_____

_____

_____

_____

_____

_____

_____

_____

_____

_____

_____

_____

_____

economize

Refer back to the description of the person you loathe
(page 46). Write a haiku about this person.

_____

_____

_____

_____

_____

_____

_____

_____

_____

_____

_____

_____

_____

_____

_____

_____

_____

_____

_____

Refer back to the description of the person you love (page 47).
Write a haiku about this person.

_____

_____

_____

_____

_____

_____

_____

_____

_____

_____

_____

_____

_____

_____

_____

_____

_____

haiku rules

A haiku is a three-line poem consisting of seventeen syllables total: The first line has five syllables, the second line has seven syllables, and the final line has five syllables.

Make a list of different styles of walking. Sit in a public place and observe all the ways that people move—note pace, posture, how they swing their arms, and how they angle their feet.

stroll, amble, streak

_____   _____
_____   _____
_____   _____
_____   _____
_____   _____
_____   _____
_____   _____
_____   _____
_____   _____
_____   _____
_____   _____
_____   _____
_____   _____
_____   _____
_____   _____
_____   _____
_____   _____
_____   _____
_____   _____
_____   _____
_____   _____

walk the line

Watch a bunch of different people doing exactly the same thing (e.g., going through the checkout line at the grocery store or catching their train at a busy station). Write a scene in which you differentiate the people by their bodies, posture, and gait. Do not describe their faces.

the revealing object

What we feel the need to hide reveals something about our core selves. What do the following hypothetical scenarios reveal about your own character?

A new romantic interest is coming over for dinner. What objects do you put out of sight?

_____

_____

_____

_____

_____

_____

_____

You're unloading your groceries and stow a few things in the top cabinet, out of view. What are they?

_____

_____

_____

_____

_____

_____

_____

Your mother is coming over to help you pack your apartment for a move. What do you box up before she arrives?

_____

_____

_____

_____

_____

_____

_____

Your partner is away for the weekend and you have total control of all media. What do you watch on TV (or what music do you listen to)?

_____

_____

_____

_____

_____

_____

_____

same dude, different crew

Describe a teenage boy's manner, behavior, and thoughts at a birthday party for his grandmother.

_____

_____

_____

_____

_____

_____

_____

_____

_____

_____

_____

_____

_____

_____

_____

_____

_____

_____

_____

_____

_____

Describe the same boy out with his friends later,
skateboarding.

_____

_____

_____

_____

_____

_____

_____

_____

_____

_____

_____

_____

_____

_____

_____

_____

_____

_____

_____

Take time to observe people's hands—their size, shape, texture, and gestures. Keep a list of descriptive words for hands.

all thumbs, claw, gnarled

hands-on

Imagine a group of people doing an activity together that involves their hands (playing cards, quilting, or packing boxes for a move). Bring your characters to life through your description of their hands and how they use them.

_____

_____

_____

_____

_____

_____

_____

_____

_____

_____

_____

_____

_____

_____

_____

_____

_____

_____

_____

_____

identical in every way?

Think of an identical twin set you know (or siblings who look very similar, or perhaps someone who is a carbon copy of a parent). Write a description of each person, doing your utmost to distinguish the two and honor their exceptional natures and behaviors.

look closer!

For this exercise, you really have to get past the people's faces or you're going to get stuck. Think about their walking and talking styles. Think about which one would answer a question first and which one would hang back. Which one is warmer and which colder?

killing clichés

Remember "John Thune a loping gazelle, Jim Bunning a maddened grizzly" from the foreword (page 8)? Turn the following clichés into fresh metaphors to describe a new student in your class (or a new coworker, or a new member of your volunteer group).

Big as a house

_____

_____

_____

_____

Sharp as a tack

_____

_____

_____

_____

Iron-fisted

_____

_____

_____

_____

Right as rain

_____

_____

_____

_____

_____

Squeaky wheel

_____

_____

_____

_____

_____

Sly fox

_____

_____

_____

_____

_____

we need a hero

Invent the superhero that you feel the world needs right now, starting with a one-sentence tagline (e.g., "Faster than a speeding bullet . . ."). Take that short description and develop a more complicated character sketch.

_____

_____

_____

_____

_____

_____

_____

_____

_____

_____

_____

_____

_____

_____

_____

_____

_____

_____

_____

_____

_____

_____

start with the backstory

What is the superhero's name and origin story? Aside from using her special powers, what is her motivation? What are her fears, weaknesses, or limitations? What does she do when she isn't in superhero mode?

morning in the life of . . .

Describe the morning rituals of each of the following well-known characters.

Cleopatra

_____

_____

_____

_____

_____

Scarlett O'Hara

_____

_____

_____

_____

_____

Darth Vader

_____

_____

_____

_____

_____

Shakespeare

_____

_____

_____

_____

_____

Oprah

_____

_____

_____

_____

_____

Gandhi

_____

_____

_____

_____

_____

Make a point of noticing people's eyes, then compose a list of descriptive words for them, including size, shape, color, expression, physical movements, and metaphors. Flip through magazines and watch TV in search of even more eyes.

squinty, wide-eyed, weary

_____   _____
_____   _____
_____   _____
_____   _____
_____   _____
_____   _____
_____   _____
_____   _____
_____   _____
_____   _____
_____   _____
_____   _____
_____   _____
_____   _____
_____   _____
_____   _____
_____   _____
_____   _____
_____   _____

eyes can't lie

Describe your mother (or anyone you know very well) in these various emotional states. Focus on how her eyes express how she feels.

When she is exhausted

_____

_____

_____

_____

When she is confused

_____

_____

_____

_____

When she feels contrite

_____

_____

_____

_____

When she is delighted

_____

_____

_____

_____

_____

When she is empathetic

_____

_____

_____

_____

_____

When she feels sentimental

_____

_____

_____

_____

_____

believe me!

A young teenager is admiring a nail polish display in a drugstore. She's thinking about which color she'll buy once she gets her allowance. Describe her behavior, body language, and state of mind in this moment.

_____

_____

_____

_____

_____

_____

_____

_____

_____

_____

_____

_____

_____

_____

_____

_____

_____

_____

_____

As this same girl is about to leave the store, a manager accuses her of shoplifting from the cosmetics aisle. How does she feel and behave after this accusation?

_____

_____

_____

_____

_____

_____

_____

_____

_____

_____

_____

_____

_____

_____

_____

_____

winners and losers

Describe the gold medalist's manner right after winning an
Olympic event—from the point of view of the bronze medalist.

_____

_____

_____

_____

_____

_____

_____

_____

_____

_____

_____

_____

_____

_____

_____

_____

_____

_____

_____

Describe the same moment from the gold medalist's
perspective.

_____

_____

_____

_____

_____

_____

_____

_____

_____

_____

_____

_____

_____

_____

_____

_____

_____

getting in

Write the thoughts of a bike messenger delivering a package to a white-shoe law firm. The messenger has recently been accepted to Harvard Law School.

spinning gold out of lead

Write a résumé for an ex-con, taking his crimes and spinning them as accomplishments.

_____

_____

_____

_____

_____

_____

_____

_____

_____

_____

_____

_____

_____

_____

_____

_____

_____

_____

_____

_____

Pay attention to how people speak
and how their voices convey emotion.
On the facing page make a list of
verbs related to speaking (particularly
those that convey tone or volume).

mumbled, stuttered, spat

mirror, mirror

Write the inner monologue of these characters as they look at their reflections in the bathroom mirror.

A life coach

_____

_____

_____

_____

_____

_____

_____

_____

A retired marathoner

_____

_____

_____

_____

_____

_____

_____

_____

A mail carrier

_____

_____

_____

_____

_____

_____

_____

A president

_____

_____

_____

_____

_____

_____

_____

_____

_____

a description of physicality

Revisit your favorite books and magazine articles. Find an
excellent description of physicality (i.e., a character's body,
movement, and mannerisms) and copy it here.

_____

_____

_____

_____

_____

_____

_____

_____

_____

_____

_____

_____

_____

_____

_____

_____

_____

_____

_____

- Your favorite words

- Your favorite phrases

- Any unexpected turns
  in the description

repurpose a description

Borrowing the general structure from the character description that you've copied on the previous page, describe a roommate, friend, or family member doing something physical (taking out the garbage, arguing with the pizza delivery guy, etc.).

_____

_____

_____

_____

_____

_____

_____

_____

_____

_____

_____

_____

_____

_____

_____

_____

_____

fresh eyes

You've likely seen your roommate, friend, or family member a million times. Try to look at him as a stranger, studying his hands, face, twitches, and mannerisms as though you are seeing him for the first time.

drilling past the surface

Write a quick, superficial sketch of your most memorable high school teacher.

_____

_____

_____

_____

_____

_____

_____

_____

_____

_____

_____

_____

_____

_____

_____

_____

_____

_____

_____

Now drill into one of the details you shared about your teacher and make it the most significant and powerful aspect of the teacher's character.

_____

_____

_____

_____

_____

_____

_____

_____

_____

_____

_____

_____

_____

_____

_____

_____

_____

_____

shifting perspective

Three colleagues are having lunch together. One of them just got a promotion and is telling the other two about it. Describe this person from the perspective of one of the colleagues, who is jealous of his coworker's accomplishment.

Now rewrite the description of the career-advancing character from the perspective of the other colleague, who has played a mentorship role and takes pride in her coworker's accomplishment.

_____

_____

_____

_____

_____

_____

_____

_____

_____

_____

_____

_____

_____

_____

_____

_____

_____

_____

that guy

Imagine the life story of a person you see every day but don't know very well. Use physical details to convey psychological ones.

_____

_____

_____

_____

_____

_____

_____

_____

_____

_____

_____

_____

_____

_____

_____

_____

_____

_____

_____

_____

_____

_____

Designer: Debbie Berne
Project Managers: Meghan Ward and Danielle Svetcov
Art Director: Diane Shaw
Editor: Karrie Witkin
Production Manager: Rebecca Westall

ISBN: 978-1-4197-3832-6

Foreword © 2019 Constance Hale
Text © 2019 The Grotto, LLC
Cover illustrations: Svetlana Prikhnenko/Shutterstock, Lazuin/Shutterstock
Cover © 2019 Abrams

Special thanks to: Alicia Tan, Alissa Greenberg, Ashley Albert, Audrey Ferber,
Beth Winegarner, Bonnie Tsui, Bridget Quinn, Caroline Paul, Celeste Chan,
Chris Colin, Christopher Cook, Constance Hale, Diana Kapp, Elizabeth Stark,
Frances Stroh, Grace Prasad, Hunter Oatman-Stanford, Jane Ciabattari,
Jaya Padmanabhan, Jenny Bitner, Jesus Sierra, Kathryn Ma, Kristen Cosby,
Laura Fraser, Lindsey Crittenden, Lisa Gray, Lisa Hix, Lisa Lerner, Liza Boyd,
Lyzette Wanzer, Mark Wallace, Mary Ladd, Maury Zeff, Maw Shein Win,
Paul Drexler, Shanthi Sekaran, Stephanie Losee, Thaisa Frank, Todd Oppenheimer,
Vanessa Hua, Yukari Kane, Zahra Noorbakhsh

Printed and bound in China

10 9 8 7 6 5 4 3 2 1

Abrams Noterie products are available at special discounts when purchased
in quantity for premiums and promotions as well as fundraising or educational
use. Special editions can also be created to specification. For details, contact
specialsales@abramsbooks.com or the address below.

Abrams Noterie® is a registered trademark of Harry N. Abrams, Inc.

ABRAMS The Art of Books
195 Broadway, New York, NY 10007
abramsbooks.com

MIX
Paper from
responsible sources
FSC™ C144853